Out of the Closet
Into God's Arms

Out of the Closet Into God's Arms

For Teens and Adults

By Sylvia D. Huerta

To order additional copies of this book, contact:
Xlibris Corporation
1-888-795-4274
www.Xlibris.com
Orders@Xlibris.com
47009

Contents

Acknowledgement

I want to acknowledge all who struggle with homosexuality. This book is for you and your family. May God give you the courage to step out and own the freedom He has given you through His love and the sacrifice of His one and only Son Jesus Christ. He has come to set us free. For many years, those who have come to Christ have received their freedom through God's merciful unconditional love with the unfolding truth of His Word. I would like to thank God the Father for the courage and inspiration to write this book and the people He sent to nudge me on. Glory to God in the highest. My gratitude goes out to my husband for all his patience with me and the many hours he spent caring for our little one's without me. You honestly are a great man. I want to thank our Pastors Jim and Tamara Graff for being amazing leaders of Faith Family Church in Victoria, Texas. For years, the both of you have been great examples to my family. Thank you for holding up the Gospel faithfully. My appreciation also goes out to Pastor Larry Helms for giving me advice and enlightening me to dig deeper and reach farther, bless you Pastor. Thank you, my friend Rhonda Hayes for your help along with all the cappuccino I could ever want, what a friend you have always been. Margie Ruiz may God richly bless you for praying this book to come to pass. Much gratitude goes to Judy Hahn who tidied up for me, "dotting the I's and crossing the T's." Dale Goynes, thank you for getting me started with your words of confirmation and godly encouragement. I also want to thank Michelle Adams for rolling up her sleeves and sharing her wisdom to help construct this book. May God bless you all! Each one of you have been instruments of God carefully chosen to bring this all together. I love you and I thank you.

In Christ,
Mrs. Sylvia D. Huerta

Chapter 1

Living With A Deceptive Heart

For as long as I can remember, starting in the first grade, I had a girlfriend. I never gave a thought as to whether the desire for a person of the same sex meant anything to anyone but me. After all, this was my life. It was in my hands.

I had always thought that I was a good kid. I came from a good home with wonderful parents, and aside from an occasional spanking, I never suffered any physical abuse.

We had gone to a Catholic Church the early part of my childhood, but for some reason unknown to me we stopped attending and I don't recall us ever going back. Even though we weren't a religious family, I remember seeing my mom on her knees and hearing her pray in her room at night.

Even though we didn't go to church, I considered myself a good person after all being gay wasn't a crime. Knowing that it seemed right and it felt good was enough for me. No one ever said that I should be attracted to the opposite sex or that life just wasn't supposed to be that way. It was MY life and I was going to live it MY way. I just wanted to be happy. It became natural, as I grew older, to love someone of the same sex.

My parents never knew of my secret until I was the age of nineteen. At that time my mother received a phone call from the mother of my high school girlfriend. She had found out somehow. My parents weren't happy about it either. Dad, in his disappointment, clearly disapproved and my mother was noticeably discouraged. Even though I knew that they still loved me whatever the situation, my heart sank to see their looks of disappointment. We never discussed what it might have meant to God. I didn't think that it meant anything to God anyway. I did know one thing; I had to live my life the best way for me. So I moved away from my parents.

In 1981, at age 19, I left my hometown of Port Lavaca to join my friends in Victoria, a city probably three times as big. I had already frequented the gay nightclubs in Victoria so I was familiar with most of the crowd. I had the time of my life. This was what I called life. This was the way for me.

Jesus tells us in John 14:6, "I am the way, the truth, and the life. No one comes to the Father except through me." How could He be the way, the truth, and the life for me? If He says that He is the way and that He is the life and I'm living life the way that pleases me, are these two ways of life the same? And what did He mean by claiming to be the truth? I honestly didn't know anything about this language of the Bible.

I've heard myself speak the words "God loves me just the way I am. He's a loving God. It shouldn't matter how I'm living as long as I'm happy and I'm not hurting anybody. So no matter how I choose to live my life God will love me forever." It is true. God loves us. He can't stop loving His creation. 1 John 4:16 says, "God is love." The love in God's eyes has the awesome capability to see us pure, to see us innocent, to see us without the soil of sin on our bodies. God has a deep love for His creation, making available the very best for us, desiring for us to have a completely prosperous life.

In 1985, my sister Margie invited me to go to church with her. She was a member of Faith Family Church in Victoria. I remember the patience my sister had with me. She never made me feel guilty because of my lifestyle. She never talked down to me or criticized me. I can recall now how she kept quite and allowed the Lord to take care of all suggestions and convictions in my life. That says a lot for someone whom I am sure was praying for the move of God in my life. There I was in church with her and it felt strange. Within myself I felt so out of place. A misfit was more like a word that fit me. I didn't know it then, but **God was there and all that mattered to Him was that I was there**. He was glad to see me and welcomed me with an open heart. **It doesn't matter where we've been or what we've done, He's just glad we came to visit.** I don't remember everything the preacher said, but I do remember that I cried uncontrollably while everyone sang during praise and worship. There was a strong Godly presence in the place that I could not deny. One that had the power to touch the core of my being. One that made me feel like I was the only one in His holy presence. His eyes could see right through me past all my homosexual desires. Yet, He loved me freely. I belonged to Him. No matter the route I had taken in my life, I knew I belonged to Him. In Psalm 139:7,8 we can read, "Where can I go from your Spirit? Where can I flee from your presence? If I go up to the heavens, you are there; if I make my bed in the depths, you are there." Approachable and accessible is the God of all generations. He makes His grace available in all situations.

When I arrived home that night, I felt confused. My live-in girlfriend of five years said that I was acting strange. That was to say the least about how I felt.

I couldn't explain what I didn't know, but I had been affected somehow. The feeling was new to me. I couldn't even sleep at night. The touch of a different Presence was with me. His presence was advancing upon me without hate and without prejudice against the homosexual environment of my home. He had followed me home. His unconditional love was embracing me in the middle of my life of twenty six years of lesbianism.

For days I prayed off and on to God, asking Him to give me a sign about whether my life was right or wrong. Why was I questioning it now? I had never questioned it before. I was so sure of myself and of who I was for so many years but now the table was turning on me to give me a different perspective about life. Perhaps I was beginning to open my eyes to the reality of a supernatural God who's interest in my daily life was deeper than any relationship I had ever had. Even though my conscience was bothering me, I was still hoping for a definite approval from God on my same sex relationship because I didn't want to leave my life as a lesbian.

Why couldn't I be gay? Why not live out the love I had in me just the way a heterosexual could? I had a right to fulfill my own desires.

One night, with my lover lying asleep next to me, I had a dream. I saw for the first time what looked like Jesus. He was sitting next to me by my bed. I strained to look at Him. He was so beautiful. He was so bright. I wasted no time in seeking his approval to love this woman lying next to me. I really thought this spiritual being in front of me was Jesus. It looked like Him anyway. Intently, I waited for an answer. He didn't say a word, but gracefully he nodded his head in approval. If I had just opened the Bible, God the Father would have given me the answer Himself. Although, after reading the truth, would I have believed it? Would I have believed that Satan the master of deception, the father of lies was behind it all? Would I have believed that homosexuality was never God's intent?

Well, it's easy to say that we believe, but believing is accepting a certain thing as the truth and possessing that truth in our heart. I believe it's called faith. How could I have accepted God's word in my life if from childhood my mentality and my thoughts were that of an active homosexual and that was where my heart was? Just how far was my heart from God anyway? Really, at that time I didn't know, but I have learned this: A person's life can be so far from God never giving Him a thought, but the moment we call on Him, we find Him already near us with arms open to receive us. "Surely the arm of the Lord is not too short to save, nor His ear to dull to hear." (Isaiah 59:1) For He stands with attention right by our side.

The next party I hosted gave me the opportunity to tell my friends about the dream of how some one that looked like Jesus had given me a sign of approval on our lifestyles. To this day, I regret even mentioning the dream. It was a mistake. Whether they believed me or not, I really didn't know, but what I did know was that the Lord existed, and I knew that He was sovereign. I just hadn't known where I stood with Him.

As the years went by, I had my share of relationships, some lasting longer than others. It wasn't until the last relationship I was in that my life turned around. It was hard for me to let go when she announced that we were through. This relationship made a lasting effect on me.

To tell the truth, it all seemed like a bad dream. I felt so obsessed in the relationship that I was miserable trying to make myself happy. I was happy because we were together, but unhappy because the love we had for one another was not mutual. I had a tormenting passion that kept me awake crying in my own darkness. I definitely did not want to let go even though I knew it was over. There was no way that I could imagine my life without her nor did I care to, but I did the only thing that I could do, I found myself a small apartment and proceeded to move out.

I could have ended my life and ended all the turmoil that I was feeling, but that wasn't the answer. No, I couldn't do that to myself. I knew that something had to give way. My calloused life was going to have to get better than this at one point or another. Maybe she would come back, or maybe in time I would get over this sad dilemma. I just knew my life had to get better. I began to question, "Was this all there was to life?" Well, it certainly couldn't get any worse for me. They say once you hit bottom there's nowhere else but up. Well, I guess for a person who wanted to keep going that expression would hold to be true. I wallowed in my sorrow for a while. I would get consolation from my friends, and then I would drink myself to sleep. I was as miserable as a person could be, drunk every night.

Sitting in the darkness, I could feel that old restless, empty feeling stirring up inside of me that I had occasionally felt throughout my lifetime, only now it was increasingly stronger. There were many times when I wasn't aware of the reality of the presence of God that was around me. All I could feel was the lonely darkness that reminded me of the dead end road I had come upon. Psalm 34:18 says, "The Lord is close to the brokenhearted and saves those who are crushed in spirit." He was there all along, loving me and reaching out to me, but I never knew it. I was too tangled up, too deeply involved in my circumstances to notice my God. He was well aware of the war in my soul. He felt everything that I felt and longed to fill that surging turmoil with His mercy and calm peace, the peace that only Jesus would give. I didn't know that I needed to surrender and lay my heart down before Him at the cross so that I could take Him up on this peace He had for me.

Let me tell you something about this wretched heart that led me directly into the wilderness of this lonely and miserable life.

In the silent darkness of everyone's heart lies the effect of past experiences in life. Although, they may be old and covered up memories, they are powerful enough to become the enemies that ultimately deliver destruction into our present lives.

The inner walls of the chambers of my heart were painted several different times. The pigment was mixed with school day embarrassments and memories of a shocked and upset junior high schoolteacher. She had kept me after class to discipline me after taking possession of and reading a love letter that I had written to a young lover girl. Then there were the high school girls in the hallways that stared at me in despise, whispering loud enough for me to hear them critically calling me a lesbian as they walked by. Even the guys avoided me. And most of all I remembered the adulthood lover relationships that ended without hope.

Among the painted walls was an old coat of physical abuse and violence that was applied during the flaming rage of a lover's anger. I knew that she loved me. She showed that she cared, but sometimes after the all night booze parties were over, and every one went home, the darkness of alcohol, furious anger, and violence would leave me wounded, depressed, and confused. The pain on the inside was greater than the hurt on the outside. As I drove away speeding on an overpass, a thought flashed through my mind of quickly turning the car through the guardrail and soaring down to my deadly fate. I was so frustrated and distressed that such a tightly woven relationship would end up unraveled by alcohol, anger, and abuse.

The second wall was decorated with rejection and denial, trimmed with a pale color of loneliness. This relationship, which appeared to be perfect and promising, left me feeling rejected and unworthy. Though I felt so loved at the beginning of our affair, she soon lost interest in me and within a short couple of years I was denied her love and companionship, allowing myself to live in a prison of intentional neglect and intimate deprivation. I was alone surrounded by hopelessness as if in a dungeon, sitting in the darkness. How could this have happened? I became so lonely looking for love where there was none. I was searching for something that didn't exist. I just wanted to wither away. Any part of my body could hurt and be dealt with, but when it was my heart that suffered it seemed as if there was no remedy. There seemed to be no help to ease the pain.

Nothing compares to a heart filled with anguish in the midst of calamity and desperation. I once heard someone say that he so much desired to jam his fist down his own throat, grasp his treacherous heart, and yank it out to remove the misery that overwhelmed him. What a deceiver the heart can become. A treacherous muscle that keeps pumping life to your body so that you can wallow through the depression and misery it gives to your soul. It seems that an independent heart, without the guidance and leadership of God, is alone the master of its fate never lacking destruction of its own.

The remaining two walls glistened with old resurfaced coats of self-righteousness and self-importance. I would love one for a season, leave her and love another. As long as I was happy, everything was good for me. I had too much pride to notice that I was the one who was lost. I never looked back to see the fire of the bridges that I had burned. I didn't care to stop and think about the damage that I had caused. Being hurt was a part of life that I had become familiar with.

The corridors that surrounded this boxed-in chamber were painted with several coats of unfulfilled desires, bordered with fantasy and decorated with images and pictures of myself being a male character. Many times I felt as if I was a man living in a woman's body. **Only you know about your own hidden secrets that are tucked away for your private use.** I remember during some of my relationships that I often desired to have children. But knowing that it was an impossible hope couldn't dampen the grief of wanting them.

There were no mirrors in my heart. I didn't want to see myself as others might have seen me. I didn't like thinking that just because I was gay that I might see myself as maladjusted, strange, and out of place. There was no way that I would consider myself an outcast. So what if I was a lesbian? I was human. I was a person. However, there was no doubt that my lifestyle was different.

Coming out of the closet of homosexuality was a gradual process that started immediately after high school. Growing older made it easier to accept myself, but I knew that a major part of the world still didn't accept my lesbian ways. I couldn't help but feel that for this reason I didn't belong anywhere. In the back of my mind I knew that my lifestyle was tolerated but not accepted.

Many unharmonizing chimes hung from a pitch-black ceiling in my heart. They were chimes of jealousy and anger, selfishness and arrogance. They all clamored loudly each time the heart was emotionally touched. Resentment and bitterness rang out while waiting after work hours for a certain lover to arrive, only to find her in a close and friendly conversation outside another woman's home. Being left at home alone with the expectancy of her return, I felt as if my chest would cave in when I saw the marks of intimacy on her neck. My heart would beat rapidly taking in anger and jealousy for itself, while confusion and anxiety settled in to take their places.

This heart was hollow in the middle. There was no bottom, no foundation. There was nothing to hold it up or give it any support. It was almost as if it were on its own. **Yet it lived because of the grace of God.** It continued beating day in and day out just the way it was. It was masterfully created in its rainbow décor of abuse, rejection, denial, and pride, streaked with contrasting colors of unfulfilled desires, fantasies, and secret thoughts that no one else could have known but God. Even so, my heart was still cherished and very precious to an Almighty Father who stood by loving me and beckoning me to come home to Him just as I was. He had searched my heart and understood every motive behind my thoughts (1Chronicles 28: 9). "Would not God have discovered it, since He knows the secrets of the heart?" (Psalms 44:21) **I had a heart made of deception and deceived by its own ways.**

I know how it feels to have your dreams shattered to pieces when relationships go wrong. I know how it hurts to feel alone and broken with or without friends surrounding you. I know how it feels to live just for today because tomorrow is grim and uncertain. I understand the emotions of a crushed life that come from deep within you when your heart hurts so much and all you can do is scream with all of your might to release the pressure. But I am telling you that there is a God who knows exactly what to do when you don't. He knows how to do for you when you can't, and He can do what no one else can do to give you the joy you need by His own divine hand.

It was a confirmed fact that I knew nothing of the peace that God had to offer me since I sat at the window of my little attic apartment night after night drinking, consumed with depression and restless anxiety. Time was all I knew that could help alleviate this sickening pain.

We can sit, think and wonder how we let ourselves get where we are. Maybe we don't even remember how we ended up with these homosexual tendencies. Some of us feel helpless and without a clue as to why we even feel this way. We may not have chosen this way of life. Maybe unfavorable circumstances or a negative environment in which we had no control of swayed our thoughts and caused us to believe that the homosexual road was the better road to take, the safer road to travel.

A little booklet from a Love Won Out series that I have read titled *The Heart Of The Matter—Root Causes of Female Homosexuality* gives some primary contributing factors to the core of lesbianism. It lists that lesbianism often results from five primary conditions. And I just want to touch on them briefly to give us something to think about.

The first is the basic relationship between a mother and her daughter. There needs to be a bond between the two with the daughter perceiving her mother to be a positive female role model.

The second one is the relationship between a father and his daughter. Young daughters need affirmation of their beauty and femininity from their fathers with the daughter perceiving her father to be a positive male role model.

The third one is a dysfunctional family. A quick look at a couple of definitions from Webster's Dictionary of dysfunctional are impaired (as in damaged or injured) and incomplete. This includes negative relationships and physical abuse.

The forth one is an identity struggle. The King James Version of the Bible says in Proverbs 23:7 "as a man thinketh in his heart, so is he." The struggle control center is in our minds and hearts but greater than the struggle is the answer that we find in God's Word of Truth that unfolds the significance and purpose for our lives. Our identity comes from our Creator.

The fifth factor listed to the core of lesbianism is traumatic events. *The Heart Of The Matter* lists divorce, molestation, death in the family, incest and rape as some of these events and goes on to mention that at least eighty percent of all lesbians have been sexually violated in some way.

Pin pointing the turning point can be difficult. This is why sometimes we find ourselves saying, "I didn't choose to be this way, but this is what I am". I can relate to that completely. But if you choose and determine in your heart to get out of it, you can. No matter what the situation or circumstances were before, I have found that there is someone who can and will give hope for change in our lives. His name is Jesus. There is hope in Him alone.

Think about your own root causes but understand that we were all born sinners from the beginning. The deepest roots for us may have started from infancy or perhaps developmental childhood days but we need to understand that this sin was already here on the earth before we were born. The tricky thing about it is that you start thinking that maybe you were born gay. Of all the reading I have done about the born gay theory, I have found that scientists and professionals alike who have researched and performed different studies trying to prove this theory as being true have not been able to prove anything of the sort. What they did find was that homosexuality is indeed treatable. Well I agree. I am living proof. There is hope. Personally what I find to be true is that when I am with a loving and powerful God who knows how to raise the sinful dead from their grave environments all things are possible!

Chapter 2

I Am Not Alone

As time went on, I did all that I could to keep myself occupied. I stayed involved at work. I had a job as a security officer at a local chemical plant that kept me busy with twelve hour shifts, but when I wasn't at my job and had time to spare, that sick empty feeling would surface to the pit of my soul.

Later I started going out with a co-worker who had been interested in me. Without caring that he liked me or not, and after being asked several times to join him for a few drinks, I finally accepted his offer.

Starting at the age of seven, I had dressed as a male figure and that was how I went out with him. In my mind we were two of the same kind going out on the town. It was very natural for me because throughout my life I had chosen to dress as a man, walk as a man, think as a man, and so I considered myself a man in character.

But, no matter what I was like, this guy Frank still admired me. I had explained to him that I was gay, but he said that he had already known and that it didn't bother him at all. We became good friends as he listened to me cry and share my sorrows about the last lover I had lost.

A few months later, I realized that he was hoping to take our friendship further. He was getting serious because I had let him get too close. I quickly ran him off and told him not to bother calling me or coming over again. As we sat at my kitchen table, I recall looking into his face and watching him cry. He was sincere. I wasn't expecting that to happen, but I had to put a stop to something that I didn't know how to handle. He left and that was the end of that.

Three months later, on a Sunday morning, I awoke and turned on the television set. Alone and in my small living room, flipping through the stations, I found nothing but religious programs. Not being able to find any thing else to watch, I finally left it on a channel that had this big, blond headed guy preaching about what he called the blood of Jesus flowing like a river. Amused, I kept listening. It seemed interesting enough to me, so I sat down and made myself comfortable on the couch to hear the rest of what he had to say. I had never heard this kind of preaching before. To be honest with you, I really hadn't heard much preaching at all. My eyes were glued to the television set as if I was watching a boxing championship fight. **What I didn't know was that it was a championship fight for MY SOUL.** My ears could hear only the man's voice. I had blocked everything out of my mind as he continued to tell me to close my eyes and picture myself standing alone next to a river of blood. Then he said that this blood was the blood of Jesus Christ. From an aerial view, I could actually see myself standing all alone by this river of flowing blood that had once sustained the life of a Man Who because of His great love for us was compelled to die for all the wrong things we had ever done. Romans 5:8 tells me "God demonstrates His own love for us in this: While we were still sinners Christ died for us".

The preacher instructed me to throw my heavy burden into the river and I would then see it sink, never to be seen again. The only thing weighing heavy on my heart was this homosexual life.

He had given me an invitation to hurl in whatever problem I was facing whether it was drugs, alcohol, prostitution, suicide, depression, or lesbianism and so forth. He went on to mention more, but after he said lesbianism, I singled myself out, as if I were stepping behind a line assigned just for me.

Maybe you haven't yet experienced it for yourself, or maybe you've just started your life in homosexuality, but the gay lifestyle is not a grand and great path that one can so easily embrace. As you travel along this particular road, you will find yourself battling against possessiveness, jealousy, violence, cheating and loneliness more often than you would any other road you would have traveled. For those of you who have been gay long enough to know, you will find this to be just as I have said. Some of your personal experiences may be better or some may be worse.

I could not comprehend the way I felt, but I knew God was waiting for me with all His love and mercy and it was drawing me closer to Him like a magnet. Ephesians 2:4-5 states, "Because of His great love for us, God, who is rich in mercy, made us alive with Christ even when we were dead in transgressions-it is by grace you have been saved." He wants to show us the wonderful things that He can do with our lives, if we just give Him the opportunity. In Jeremiah 31:3-4 God tells us, "I have loved you with an everlasting love; I have drawn you with loving-kindness. I will build you up again and you will be rebuilt, O Virgin Israel. Again you will take up your tambourines and go out to dance with the joyful." I know God wants that for ALL of His people. He wants you to know that He doesn't hate you, but loves you with an everlasting love and wants a good life for you. He specializes in rebuilding lives. He can do it. He is willing to give you a new life through His mercy, His compassion, and His great incomparable love. God says, "Forget the former things; do not dwell on the past. See, I am doing a new thing! Now it springs up; do you not perceive it? I am making a way in the desert and streams in the wasteland." (Isaiah 43:18-19) He will make a way for you in the deadest driest part of your life. When all your plans and dreams have gone to waste, He will rain down on you streams of life.

We can choose Him or reject Him. We can be born again in our spirits or stay spiritually dead. We can have everlasting life or eternal damnation. It's our decision to make, but there are only two choices to pick from. The Bible says "Choose for yourselves this day whom you will serve" (Joshua 24:15) I believe that is what He is saying to you right now. He is giving you His hand to grab on to so that He can pull you out of where you don't need to be. He has the ability to pull you out of your darkness and into His light.

I could have reasoned with myself and said that I was born to be gay and meant to live that way, but that would have been no more the truth than as if I was already born a prostitute, a drunkard, a drug abuser, a thief, or a murderer. No, God created our inmost being, and Psalm 139:13-16 goes on to say, "You knit me together in my mother's womb. I praise you because I am fearfully and wonderfully made; your works are wonderful, I know that full well. My frame was not hidden from you when I was made in the secret place. When I was woven together in the depths of the earth, your eyes saw my unformed body." In His love, God made us a perfect workmanship of His glory, crafted by His hands, to be His loving, willing, obedient and blessed children. This is how I know that we are capable of changing and getting out of whatever type of life we are living, because we are the workmanship of God. That's how He created us. We are His. You don't have to be gay. You can change and only God has the power to do it for you if you are willing. You don't have to be bound by a tormenting heart that will eventually destroy you. You can live a blessed life because God is for you not against you. I think of the words to a favorite song of mine by Jaci Velasques that says, "When I was a little child, constantly the eyes of God watched over me." I know that God has watched over us for such a time as this. He has a purpose for your life that He has known about for years. You were made from His immeasurable love and exist for a specific and true purpose. Because of this powerful purpose, all you would do in your life would bring you joy and give honor and glory to God. All you put your hands to do would be filled with success and blessing to ultimately produce great rewards for you. **His Holy Spirit has the power we need when we are willing to overcome.**

If you put your trust in Him, His love will make the difference for you. "Many are the woes of the wicked, but the **Lord's unfailing love surrounds the man who trusts in him.**" (Psalms 32:10) "So do not fear, for **I am with you;** do not be dismayed, for **I am your God**. I will strengthen you and help you; I will uphold you with my righteous right hand." (Isaiah 41:10) He can take you to His land of healing and help keep you there. He will be your fortress and your refuge in your time of trouble. He will not fail you, because He knows the plans that He has for you are prosperous and successful with hope and a future.

He has given His only Son to die on the cross so that you might have a better life, a blessed life, an eternal life. The shed blood of Jesus is to wash you from the very thing that has kept you separated from God and give you a new start on a life reconciled to Him. That's how precious you are to Him. It doesn't matter what you think about yourself or what anyone else thinks about you. You are an esteemed and valuable person to Him, as precious to Him as the day you were conceived. He will make you an heir, a co-heir with Christ. He is for you, not against you. Take one step forward in faith and He will meet your need right where you are, just the way you are. There's no having to clean up your act or change anything before you come. Just come as you are and He will receive you.

God knew with just a little of my faith that He could move mountains. There I stood face to face with the living God. Tears were streaming down my face, as I thought of what Jesus must have looked like nailed to that old wooden cross for me. I lifted my heart that seemed too heavy to carry any longer and as if it were an old corroded anchor, I heaved all my thirty three years into the flowing river of the Lord's blood. I stood there amazed. Revelation 12:11 states, "They overcame him (Satan) by the **blood** of the Lamb and by the word of their testimony." The preacher then took the time to lead me in a prayer of repentance and assured me that I was not alone, that God was with me, and that He would not fail me.

An awful thing is the damage that I had caused, not just to myself, but to the people that God so loved. Swimming in the ocean of homosexuality, how many did I step on just to keep afloat for so long? "The heart is deceitful above all things and beyond cure. Who can understand it?" (Jeremiah 17:9)

A person could say that I might not have needed to turn to Jesus with my life if I wouldn't have let myself get into such situations. Maybe I wouldn't have turned to God had I met that certain special person that was just right for me. Straight or gay, I still would have to turn and make a decision about my relationship with my Creator. **No, because of sin even the best relationship revolves around a heart that possesses emptiness never able to be satisfied by human hands.** No matter how happy or successful a person may seem, that concealed hollow place in the heart of darkness remains unavoidably without peace and contentment as it gnaws at what little self-made pleasure one does have until Jesus is allowed to come in and take His place.

It could be for similar or different reasons your heart aches as mine did. Maybe you have that empty feeling inside that you have tried to fill with the love and expectations of others. Aside from the will of God for your life, you have tried in vain to fill in the void with what seemed promising, but it ended up being a temporary pleasure. You tried everything to reach out to happiness. You tried everything to let go of the pain, but you never have tried the one genuine love of Jesus Christ. **When you are living out of the will of God, the things you go through serve purpose to God.** The Bible tells us that our broken hearts are the perfect sacrifices that God wants and that He will not despise or look down on us with contempt. Psalms 51:17 says, "The sacrifices of God are a broken spirit; a broken and contrite heart, O God, you will not despise."

Jesus has become the solid rock of my heart's foundation. He has become the firm ground I have pitched my heart's tent upon in this journey for love. He has torn down the tainted walls of my past and constructed within me a new heart by His forgiveness and grace. He continues to color it with His own reflections. With strokes that give transformation, His divine brush dispenses the promises of His words leaving an aura of refreshing newness and the incense of sweet hope.

God the Father calls the abuser with the abused, the neglecter with the neglected, the lover and the unloved to come into His glorious presence and find rest for the soul.

A few days later, I went to my best friend's house to tell her what had happened to me. Before then I hadn't told anyone. If I could tell anyone, she would have to be the one. We were as close as sisters, and I wanted to share with her what had happened to me while it was still a recent event.

While at her house, I asked her to come out and sit in my car with me to have some privacy. I told her of my decision to live for Christ. I told her that Jesus had sacrificed Himself for our sins and that the life we were living was not going to give us eternal life in heaven. Only through repentance and accepting what Christ had done and receiving Him as Lord and Savior of our lives would we be guaranteed such a gift. My friend started crying and then became angry with me. I couldn't help but tell her the truth in the hope that she too would accept Christ as her Savior.

Slowly backing out of the driveway, I watched her walk away from me toward her front door steps. I couldn't help but feel in my heart that in some way I had lost her as the best friend I ever had.

I couldn't force her to accept Jesus. It would have to be a decision she would have to make on her own someday. "For God so loved the world that He gave His one and only Son, that whoever believes in Him shall not perish but have eternal life." (John 3:16)

He had done it for me, for my family, for my friends, and for whosoever would believe because we were that important to Him, because we meant everything to Him, because He loved us with an unfathomable, unlimited love. No matter how you live, no matter what your life is about, He loves you and no one can stop you from living a blessed significant purpose filled life on this earth and an eternal life in heaven, no one except you. "God demonstrates His own love for us in this: **While we were still sinners**, Christ died for us." (Romans 5:8) This means that while I was out in my pleasurable sin, in His affliction, He died for me. While you were out enjoying your sin, He faithfully died for you. He was concerned enough to die for you. **He was thinking of us when we weren't thinking of Him.**

Nothing can stop you except yourself, your own free will. The choice that you make or choose not to make will certainly be an eternal one. God has done all He has set out to do by nailing all our sin to the cross with Jesus and allowing Him to take all the painful punishment. God didn't want to be without you. He knew we could never be with Him unless He gave a perfect, unblemished sacrifice.

He wouldn't allow sin to come between Him and us. So, He did something about it. "For the sake of His great name the Lord will not reject His people, because **the Lord was pleased to make you His own.**" (1 Samuel 12:22) "So do not fear, for I am with you; do not be dismayed, for I am your God. I will strengthen you and help you; I will uphold you with my righteous right hand." (Isaiah 41:10).

I have to admit something to you. When I was sitting there with my eyes closed about to unload my whole life to God, I felt myself being somewhat afraid. I really didn't know what to think about it all because my past was flashing through my mind. I was thinking of all the shameful things that I had done and yet there hung this man suspended on a cross with three long, rusty nails. Shameful or not He was hanging there for me, and it didn't matter to Him what I had done in my life.

"For I am convinced that neither death nor life, neither angels nor demons, neither the present nor the future, nor any powers, neither height nor depth, nor anything else in all creation, will be able to separate us from the love of God that is in Christ Jesus our Lord." (Romans 8:38-39) I was so grateful for what my Lord had done for me. It was something that I knew I could have never done for myself. That is what God's grace is all about doing something for us that we could never do for ourselves. Trusting in God and the unconditional love that He had for me made it easier to take that step toward Him.

He drove out my enemy before me, saying, "Destroy him!" (Deuteronomy 33:27) He will drive out your enemy before you that is trying to destroy YOU! His love for you has fought the battle to keep you safe, to give you the victory, to help you overcome and stand in triumph washed by the blood of the Lamb, Jesus Christ. Lay your heart down and let God take it into His hands. While life gets to be too much for you to handle, God wants you to know that He is here for you day and night, and sees you when you're crying out in anguish, anger, and frustration. He has made a way for your victory against your enemy Satan who brings his army of poverty, disease, depression, suicide, drugs, homosexuality, and other various troops of destruction against you. God will strengthen your heart and give you hope. He says to you, "Never will I leave you; never will I forsake you." (Hebrews 13:5)

Chapter 3

Understanding The Beginning

Thinking about the whole idea of God creating us is awesome. He made us to love, to fellowship with, to institute the foundation of His family in us, to live productive lives, with purpose and significance in His honor, to walk in the coolness of the garden with Him as Adam and Eve had done. He made us in His image. His image is complete in the creation of both male and female genders to complete humanity. God's idea, God's image, He made us from His heart.

He made us so that we could have a relationship with Him. Of all the things that He had made the animals, the sea, the earth, stars, and the angels, mankind was what He made in the image of Himself. Because we are made in His image, we are a part of Him, capable of having a relationship with Him.

I think we can agree that when a person has a child, naturally he or she has a close relationship with that child and has a great interest in his life. He loves, directs, advises, disciplines, comforts, and provides for that child. When the son or daughter falls, the parent is there to lift him up. A loving parent never expects his child to go through life without his care or guidance. So it is with our Heavenly Father. However, His plans were disrupted.

When Satan deceived Eve and Adam after tempting them with the apple, they stepped out of the will of God for their lives. At that moment, through disobedience, sin flooded into the world. Satan was handed over the power to reign in the lives of the people and has been the deceiver ever since. He has injected his venomous seeds of envy, hate, suicide, murder, lust, incest, prostitution, pornography, alcoholism, fornication, adultery, depression, homosexuality, and the occult along with several different diseases, into the people that he hates the most, God's creation.

Why would he do these things? To destroy the life that God made within us, to kill our spirits and steal the blessed life God intended for us to have. Satan wants to kill any living person that has a chance of being restored to God. He hates you. In John 10:10 Jesus states, "The thief comes only to steal and kill and destroy; I have come that they may have life, and have it to the full." That is why we needed a Savior because things were messed up from the beginning. We cannot say that we are so good that we don't need God. Sin was established in our lives from the beginning of time, before we were even born.

Adam and Eve knew nothing about sin until they ate from the tree of the knowledge of good and evil. This was the tree that God had forbidden them to eat. Due to sin, death had been established, but thank God **"where sin increased, grace increased all the more."** (Romans 5:20) Just as sin delivers us unto our death, grace delivers us unto our righteousness. This is the right to eternal life in Jesus Christ our Lord.

God is unlimited as to what His grace can bring, but many times it is described as unmerited favor and undeserved love. God loves you and me because we are His creation. Even though Satan brings sin into our lives and deceives us in so many ways, (and I speak from experience) God favored us with His unconditional love. A love that no demon could EVER overpower. "For it is by grace you have been saved through faith—and this not from yourselves, it is the gift of God-not by works so that no one can boast." (Ephesians 2:8-9)

Do you think God can save you from what it is you're going through? ABSOLUTELY! **It is His will, but it has to be your will, too.** He has seen everything that you have gone through. He knows your problem and is very familiar with your hurt. He knows how far back this problem has come. He saved me and I know that He has made that possible for you. Maybe you didn't commit a sin as seriously as murder, and maybe you did. But what's so miraculous is that He still pours out His forgiveness and His gift of salvation no matter how heinous the crime. That's what salvation is all about. You can never do something so bad that He won't pardon you because He already has through His Son Jesus Christ. It's been done once and for all. It's been finished. God will never, in no way ever, go back on His word. His forgiveness is for everyone. He has always loved you in spite of yourself. He has always loved me in spite of myself. It's not about what all we've done; it's about what all Jesus did to cancel out our sin.

On the cross, He emptied His life so that you might have life and have it more abundantly. Why do I say might? Because salvation has been provided, but it's up to you to receive it as yours. Being nailed to the cross and left to die in excruciating, agonizing pain was just the beginning of the punishment. For three days, Jesus was isolated in the heart of the earth, in the pit of darkness, separated from God for the first time in His life in the bowels of hell. That should have been me down there, that should have been us, but He took our place. He took your place. He had all the power and all the authority to take the keys of death and Hades and on the third day He rose from the grave. Victory is ours.

Right this minute, there are countless people in the darkness of hell where the worm never dies but remains slithering in and out the entire soul. The fire never quenches. The blast of flames never cease. And though the stench of death fills their senses, reminding them of their fate, they didn't have to go. Jesus, Himself, foretold in Matthew 8:12 that "the subjects of the kingdom will be thrown outside, into the darkness, where there will be weeping and gnashing of teeth." He warns us with the truth because He loves us.

Jesus reveals to us in Luke 16:19-31, "There was a rich man who was dressed in purple and fine linen and lived in luxury every day. At his gate was laid a beggar named Lazarus, covered with sores and longing to eat what fell from the rich man's table. Even the dogs came and licked his sores.

"The time came when the beggar died and the angels carried him to Abraham's side. The rich man also died and was buried. In hell, where he was in torment, he looked up and saw Abraham far away, with Lazarus by his side. So he called to him, 'Father Abraham, have pity on me and send Lazarus to dip the tip of his finger in water and cool my tongue, because I am in agony in this fire.'"

"But Abraham replied, 'Son, remember that in your lifetime you received your good things, while Lazarus received bad things, but now he is comforted here and you are in agony. And besides all this, between us and you a great chasm has been fixed, so that those who want to go from here to you cannot, nor can anyone cross from there to us.'" There was nothing in between only an impassable gulf.

"He answered, 'Then I beg you, father, and send Lazarus to my father's house, for I have five brothers. Let him warn them, so that they will not also come to this place of torment.'"

"Abraham replied, 'They have Moses and the Prophets; let them listen to them.'"

"'No, father Abraham,' he said, but if someone from the dead goes to them, they will repent.'"

"He said to him, 'If they don't listen to Moses and the Prophets they will not be convinced even if someone rises from the dead'."

If he only would have believed in and lived for God, he wouldn't have been there. Every day of his life he passed up Lazarus who was sitting at his gate, and in the same way, he passed up a loving merciful Father whom he did not care to follow. Revelation 3:20 states that Jesus said, "Here I am! I stand at the door and knock. If anyone hears my voice and opens the door, I will come in and eat with him, and he with me."

The rich man lived his life without need of anything, not even a forgiving God. Notice when Abraham was speaking to him, he said, "in your lifetime you received YOUR good things." Abraham wasn't knocking the fact that the man was rich, for God wants us all to prosper. He was stating that the man had received in life what HE HAD CONSIDERED as good. Those things that the rich man had UNDERSTOOD as GOOD in his life. Those things that he ACKNOWLEDGED as VALUABLE. The rich man had EVERYTHING except the most important possession in the world, SALVATION. Jesus tells us in Matthew 16:26, "What good will it be for a man if he gains the whole world, yet forfeits his soul?" All the riches in the world couldn't save him now.

He probably wasn't that bad of a person, but one's destiny is not determined on whether that person has been good, bad or indifferent. Whether you are with or without Jesus Christ in your life determines your destination.

Ages upon ages have passed, generation upon generation has come and gone, and somewhere through time God's people have forgotten Him. They have all turned and gone their own way. Some people live day to day, year to year without the God who loves and cherishes them. Their whole lives pass them by without their ever getting to know the One who really loves them. They live, they work, and then they die without Him and where does that leave them? It leaves them in hell just like the rich man who was without God in his life.

The rich man was very much aware that he was in hell. He could feel the unquenchable fire; he could smell the unbearable stench, and in the pit of darkness he could hear the painful cries of those who accompanied him. He certainly didn't want his brothers to be there. He wanted someone to warn them. Maybe someone already had, but they were comfortable with the way things were in their lives and didn't want to be bothered. It could be that they had already heard about the kingdom of heaven, but had made a decision to put it off for a more convenient time in their lives, perhaps in their old age, or on their death bed, but who is guaranteed the luxury of a death bed? Many times death comes quickly and unexpectedly and takes you where you made yourself accountable to go. The place of hell exists, but it wasn't made for us. It was made for the devil and his angels.

How great is the love of God for you and me. There is no greater love. No one else can love you as much as God can. No one will ever love you as much as God does. His arms are open to receive all who call on His name. "The same Lord is Lord of all and richly blesses all who call on Him, for, 'Everyone who calls on the name of the Lord will be saved'." (Romans10: 12-13) "Seek the Lord while He may be found; call on Him while He is near. Let the wicked forsake his way and the evil man his thoughts. Let him turn to the Lord and He will have mercy on him, and to our God for he will freely pardon." (Isaiah 55:6-7) As soon as we turn to the Lord, like an extended blanket, His mercy covers the shame of our sin.

He is a just God who has established right and wrong. Deuteronomy 30:19-20 says, "This day I call heaven and earth as witnesses against you that I have set before you life and death, blessings and curses. Now choose life, so that you and your children may live and that you may love the Lord your God, listen to His voice, and hold fast to Him. For the Lord is your life, and He will give you many years in the land he swore to give to your fathers, Abraham, Isaac, and Jacob." He is a God of principle, but He is a God of mercy. Often times when one hears of God as being a God of justice, He is thought of as a harsh and many times unforgiving Father. The word justice, in most cases, paints a cold picture with the background of a cruel world. Although to this day He holds in effect His commands and decrees, and His offer of life or death has not changed, God remains merciful within all His justice. He is a forgiving God not wanting any one to perish. He is a God who stands beside the sacred cross of Jesus and declares the people guiltless and without shame and as we turn to Him, we see that He truly is a compassionate Father who does not hate but loves His people. From His mercy, through the work of the cross of Jesus, He helps us begin again pure and without sin giving us the Holy Spirit to lead the way.

Chapter 4

Taking Hold Of God's Will

How could I make myself right or get my life right before God? What did I need to do? Was I to decide that from this moment on I was going to be an exceptionally good person, trying not to do anything bad and live by every command and law of God? I knew there would be no way that I could succeed in my own strength. These were the questions that I would ask myself and this was what I discovered.

The Bible indicates that the laws of God were established to keep us from harm, to save us from destroying our own souls, to give us knowledge of sin, and most of all to help lead us to Christ. If I lived my life strictly upon every command in and of my own strength, I would fail. I couldn't make myself right. "Therefore no one will be declared righteous in his sight by observing the law; rather, through the law we become CONSCIOUS of sin."

"But now a righteousness from God, apart from law, has been made known, to which the Law and the Prophets testify. This righteousness from God comes through faith in Jesus Christ to all who believe. **There is no difference**, for all have sinned and fall short of the glory of God, and are justified freely by his grace through the redemption that came by Christ Jesus. God presented him as a sacrifice of atonement, through faith in his blood." Romans 3:20-25

So my righteousness would have to come through faith in Him, allowing Him, Who is the unblemished Lamb, to be the replacement for my self-righteousness. Because, **"All of us** have become like one who is unclean, and our righteous acts are like filthy rags; we all shrivel up like a leaf, and like the wind our sins sweep us away." (Isaiah 64:6) So no matter how good we try to be, we're still in need of a Savior, Who redeemed us with His blood, to make our lives right in the sight of God. There is no way that we can make ourselves righteous. There aren't any amounts of good deeds that will create the righteousness that we need in our hearts. "God made Him who had no sin to be sin for us, so that in Him we might become the righteousness of God." (2 Corinthians 5:21) Sound confusing? It's not. Take a step back and look at the overall picture. He took our place so that we could take a place in Him.

Sometimes God, in His all-knowing wisdom, does not give us a reason as to why He does or does not want for us to commit certain acts. He knows that we're capable of doing that which will bring us harm, and He knows that we're capable of doing that which will bring us blessing. But listen. Because He created us, His demands are not so far out of our reach that we simply cannot obey them. The heart that He formed in each one of us has the capability to conform to His righteous ways. We are equipped within to make His righteousness our own.

God's commands are designed to bring us blessing, not condemnation, as we apply them into our lives. So if you've never been blessed then turn and look toward God. Turn your heart toward God. You're going to have to see for yourself. You're going to have to go through it on your own, perhaps without your loved ones, perhaps without your friends. This relationship has to be between you and Him the Author and Finisher of your faith.

"And now, O Israel, what does the Lord your God ask of you, but to **fear** the Lord your God, to **walk** in all His ways, to **love** Him, to **serve** the **Lord your God with all your heart and with all your soul**, and to **observe** the Lord's commands and decrees that I am giving you today for **your own good.**" (Deuteronomy 10:12-13)

We have to rise above our past. We have to turn our backs on sin that separates us from Him. We need to let go of our own desires that entangle us in sexual sin. Past our sins there is blessing. The blood of Jesus washes the sin away and makes you holy before God. He makes you holy. Blessing comes from obedience to Him.

A Christian station radio announcer was once asked, "Why did God create a people, give them freedom to choose to live their lives the way they pleased then, as if in arrogance or selfish pride, demand for the people to turn to Him, love Him, and walk in His ways?" The announcer replied, "If after winning a championship NBA game, the winning team then retreating to the locker room, would demand their trophy would you think of them as prideful or selfish?" The announcer couldn't have used a better word than trophy. Webster's Dictionary gives one definition of trophy as **something taken from the enemy** and kept as a memorial of victory, as captured arms. You belong to God. Does He deserve you? Yes. Is He worthy of you? Yes. But are you willing to give yourself to Him? He is saying "Come home; I love you and I know what's best for you. I have good things in store for you."

The last words of this scripture say, "for your own good." It's for our own good. A tail of results follows all choices. There are things that we choose to do in our lives that bring bad consequences if we don't restrain ourselves from doing them.

God is the creator of love in our hearts, but who we give it to will never be His choice to make. God has had nothing to do with the direction in which you or I have taken to fulfill that desire. He is not responsible for our sexual orientation.* I am not saying that living a heterosexual life will never subject you to any negative circumstance. There is potential for negative circumstances in ANY kind of life one lives. I am saying, though, that if you will direct your love FIRST to Jesus and choose to live in the ways of God, He will bring you victory in whatever dilemma you may be in.

The Bible says that in all things God works for the good of those who love him, and are called according to his purpose. (Romans 8:28) God does not demand that a person be healed, heterosexually oriented, or happy. God demands holiness. Michael Saia, the author of the book, *Counseling The Homosexual*, wrote, "the person can choose to be holy, receive healing, and move toward heterosexual orientation as a result of His holiness." God wants us to choose to be holy people, to be holy as He is holy (Leviticus 11:44 and 20:7). He wants for us to be holy, pure, and set apart for His divine love. IN ALL THINGS He will work for the good of those who love Him, and are called according to His purpose.

What is holiness exactly? To be holy is to be spiritually pure, devoted to God, set apart from sin, and set apart in our hearts. **The** Holy Spirit reveals and manifests holiness within a person's heart, and like a salve, begins to heal the hurt with life changing results. God's word says, "Let those who love the Lord hate evil, for He guards the lives of His faithful ones and delivers them from the hand of the wicked. Light is shed upon the righteous and joy on the upright in heart." (Psalms 97:10,11) The word of God tells us to shun evil or to hate evil is to fear (respect, be in awe of) the Lord. In loving God and being faithful to Him, He promises to guard our lives and deliver us from evil harm. He sheds His light on us and brings fullness of joy in our hearts. God is so good to us, but sometimes we don't notice it. It's easy to take advantage of His goodness when you're used to doing things on your own and all you see are the things that you're doing for yourself in your own strength. We can't even order our next breath or command our next heartbeat without the hand of God as our hidden source. And that's enough to worship Him right there. And, if we **were** to ask, "God you've done so much for me, you've been so good, what can I do for you?" He would say, "**Just love me with all your heart, soul, mind, and strength.**" (Mark 12:30)

Reading your Bible and spending time in getting to know God can help us learn exactly what it is that God portrays as evil. Though hating sin is a result of fearing the Lord in this world, our lives can grow accustomed to the existence of evil and our conscience no longer be affected by its presence. So we need to go back to God's word and redefine the meanings of sin and holiness for ourselves. Establishing the truth of God's word in our hearts can quicken our conscience and help us to stay on course with God and continue life with Him in wisdom and in truth through Christ Jesus.

God's word encourages us to live by faith in His grace because we are justified by faith. We can say that to be justified would be just as if we had never sinned. That would make you a righteous person through justification by faith in what Jesus had done by the shedding of His blood. The blood of Jesus covers all unrighteousness. Colossians 1:20 claims that God " . . . reconciled to himself all things, whether things on earth or things in heaven, by making peace through His blood, shed on the cross." So then, "I do not set aside the grace of God, if righteousness could be gained through the law, Christ died for nothing!" (Galatians 2:21) Which brings us back to how to be righteous before the sight of God.

Let me point out to you that a peaceful, righteous, holy, and faithful life CANNOT be obtained through our own strength or deeds, but ONLY from the powerful presence of the Holy Spirit of Jesus residing in our hearts. Knowledge, wisdom, and deeds are incapable of bringing you a godly life without the **Holy Spirit and the Word of God.**

When I received Jesus as my personal Savior, I took a step of faith. It was like jumping off the edge of my own life and on to His foundation. I had to have faith in what Jesus had done for me was what I needed in my life to be righteous before God.

Jesus was now going to be my righteousness, but I needed to live by faith. Habakkuk 2:4 and Galatians 3:11 both read God saying, **"The righteous will live by faith."** So then by faith we will live the truth of the Word of God. Where does our faith come from? The Bible says that God Himself is the Author and Perfecter of our faith and that He has given everyone the measure of faith. So everyone starts off with the measure and it grows by hearing the word of God.

James 2:20 states that "faith without deeds is useless." I can have faith that my car can take me where I need to go, but if I never apply my faith by getting into it, turning the key, and driving off, then it would be dead and of no use. So my faith has to be accompanied by action. This is not faith in the spiritual realm. This example is faith in the natural. It is faith in something that you CAN see. Having faith in what a car is capable of doing is not to compare with the supernatural faith in what our supreme God can and will do in our lives. What I am stressing here is the WORK or ACTION that is needed to PROVE the faith one possesses. I'm saying faith must be evidence that is present in our lives because of the love we have for God. **"Faith expresses itself through love."** (Galatians 5:6)

When we believe in Jesus, we believe in everything that He stands for and in everything that He represents. Remember that believing is accepting a certain thing as the truth in our heart. **So if one believes in Jesus and in the truth that He stands for, that belief being grounded in our hearts by**

faith should be expressed in our lives by the way we live. If not, then faith without works is dead.

At the moment that you receive Christ as your Savior, the Holy Spirit, the presence of God, comes to take residence in your heart. God says, "I will give you a **new heart** and put a **new spirit** in you; I will remove from you your heart of stone and give you a heart of flesh." (Ezekiel 36:26) He empowers us with strength to live a righteous life in truth. Not expecting for us to be perfect, He works in us His perfection from that day forward as we live for Him. In Philippians 3:12, Paul, the author, tells us, "Not that I have already obtained all this, or have already been made perfect, but I **press on** to take hold of that for which Christ Jesus took hold of me." We aren't perfect; we just press on.

One night I had a dream that there was much commotion coming from the kitchen. In my dream I began walking toward that noise of confusion, and to my surprise my old friend, Frank, was standing in the middle of the kitchen shouting at me to stay out! What I saw was totally demonic. My cabinet doors had been ripped open. I watched in shock, as some raging satanic force was purposefully throwing pots and pans at him. And to my surprise, He stood there catching every utensil with his bare hands. I thought, "God what is this?" How unexplainable the spiritual world must be for us.

All this time in my life, I had exchanged the truth of God for a lie, and worshiped and served created things rather than the Creator, who is forever praised (Romans 1:25). So I kept reading my Bible. Every day on my couch, I would curl up with the Word of God letting Him transform my heart. And as I worshiped Him in song and in prayer, I could feel His very presence in the room with me. He was sweet. He was powerful. But, He was gentle.

I had plenty of leisure time after work and on weekends. My friends had long since stopped visiting me. But it was an opportunity for me to spend time in the presence of the Lord and learn more about Him.

Some time later, I had another dream. I used to have a beautiful male cat named Lokie. He was with me for seven years. Even though he loved to rub his body against me and be petted, he never cared to be held. He loved me, though he liked his space. If he slept on the bed with me, he would sleep at my feet, never by my face or at my side. Well, this one night I slept wishing that I could have been able to open my eyes.

I could hear extremely loud music, strong singing, vulgar shouting, and the hissing and howling of my cat. To tell you the truth, it was a lot of noise that woke me that night. I could feel Lokie lying on my stomach, which I knew was very odd. He had never done that before. My eyes were tightly closed, and as much as I tried to open them, I couldn't. In the natural realm, I couldn't see him, but I could see what God wanted for me to see in the spiritual realm. Why I couldn't open my eyes, only God knows. My courageous cat was looking up to the right of where I lay at a row of hideous demons standing above me in mid air. They were hissing and spitting and cursing obscenities as foul as I have never heard. My cat, in return, was hissing and growling at them. Although his action was directed to them, the demons protests were being aimed to the left of me where there stood above me a line of tall and strong holy angels like I had never seen before. They were loudly praising and worshiping God. Their praises were drowning out the frustrated defeated protests of the demons. In a small fraction, God had shown me the seriousness of the spiritual world. I knew that my soul had been set free.

I continued to meet with God each day, talking to Him and reading all about Him from my Bible. I had committed myself to attending church and going forward with my new life in Christ no matter who it *identified me with or separated me from* (Pastor John Osteen). I knew that being without Him I would fail, so I stayed close to Him and never looked back. As I remained in His presence, He was faithful to work in my heart restoring and reforming that which the devil had left as wreckage. Precious to the Lord are the broken pieces of your heart. With His gentle hands He carefully picks up every fragment, every piece. With His great love, He places them ever so carefully before Him. In His refuge, He gives great hope to the wounded and creates new life.

Chapter 5

Giving Me A New Life

I kept my trust in God, relying on His great wisdom and omniscience. I had given Him my heart and as a result I was expecting something better to become of my life. I didn't know how He was going to do it, but He had promised me eternal life and by His Spirit He had made a deposit in me that was to produce fruit. Galatians 5:22-23 states, "The fruit of the Spirit is love, joy, peace, patience, kindness, goodness, faithfulness, gentleness, and self-control. Love, I had lost. Joy, I had needed desperately. I had been overwhelmed by restlessness instead of peace, and because of that I didn't have any self-control. That was half of them so far with much needed improvement on the rest. Only God could have done it. Luke 1:37 tells us, "Nothing is impossible with God!"

Months had passed before I had gone to God and told Him, "Lord, I don't want to go against your word or disappoint you, but I sure would like a companion to share my life with and to laugh with again." Softly I heard Him say, "What happened to Frank?" I thought for a while and then gave my reply, "God, you brought me this far, and well, I guess you can take me down that route, too."

I didn't know where to start. I had no idea how to begin. It was going to be very different. I had done some crazy things during my days of darkness, but in my past life I would have never had the ability in my heart to have a serious relationship with the opposite sex. Philippians 3:13-14 states, " . . . but one thing I do: Forgetting what is behind and straining toward what is ahead, I press on toward the goal to win the prize for which God has called me heavenward in Christ Jesus." God had enabled me mentally and spiritually. He had taken my old desires away when He had torn down the walls of my tainted heart. He had replaced all the evil in my heart with His Holy Spirit that dwelled inside of me, giving me the strength to do what I needed to do. No longer did the things of darkness or the master of darkness have a hold in me.

His love is so great for us that He looks past our faults, mistakes, and incapabilities, and provides a way where there is no way. In His mercy, He crowns us with righteousness that we don't deserve and allows us to inherit His kingdom. And in His mercy, He wants to crown you too. 1Corinthians 6:9-11 soberly says, "Do you not know that the wicked will not inherit the kingdom of God? Do not be deceived: Neither the sexually immoral, nor idolators, nor adulterers, nor male prostitutes, nor **homosexual offenders**, nor thieves, nor the greedy, nor drunkards, nor slanderers, nor swindlers will inherit the kingdom of God. And this is what some of you were. But you were **washed**, you were **sanctified**, you were **justified** in the name of the Lord Jesus Christ and by the Spirit of our God." I know that scripture hurts. I'm speaking from experience. Don't close this book up yet. God has something good for you.

Notice this scripture states "this is what some of you were". In answer to the question "Is it possible to change?" People have been changing their way of living for years. Homosexuality was present in Bible time and according to this scripture people have been washed, sanctified, and justified from it over and over again. It's a matter of choice. We may not have chosen to be in this homosexual lifestyle but we certainly can choose to get out.

In this passage of scripture, He is speaking to those of us who **choose** to hold on to the gay lifestyle. It cannot be possible for the kingdom of God to live in the body of a destructive life. The kingdom of God is life to WHOSOEVER takes hold of it, but they MUST let go of the sins that ultimately bring death. **We cannot live our lives just any way we want to and expect for God to accept and approve of it on the basis of His unconditional love.** If we could live our lives any way we wanted to, then Jesus would have been a victim of murder and not a sacrifice for our sins. No, it is because of His unconditional love that He wants to take us out of our corrupt lives and **wash us, sanctify us**, and **call us justified** in the name of His Son Jesus.

God speaks to each one of us from His unconditional love. He doesn't want for us to be ignorant (and that's not a bad word) of the devil's many devices. He wishes for everyone to be saved and that includes YOU. In this passage of scripture, God is not condemning you. He is not blaming you for how you feel or what you think about another person of the same sex. You are not guilty for your feelings or desires. (M. Saia) Let me make something clear to you. God knows that Satan's battlefield is in the mind as he fights to take possession of you. If you allow him, Satan can and will influence you into sinning against God. But like I said that's IF YOU ALLOW HIM TO. **The devil's continual influence is a masterful but subtle move with a specific intention of keeping your heart turned away from God as he gains full ownership.** You alone are responsible for submitting to that influence. (M. Saia) Satan only has as much influence and power over you as you give him. Having feelings and desires contrary to God's word is not a sin until you allow it to nest in your mind and become a committed act. That's why in 2 Corinthians 10:5 God warns us to take every thought captive that sets itself up against His knowledge. We need to be careful what we think about and make those thoughts obedient to Christ. Forewarning us in Philippians 4: 8, the Bible tells us to think on good things, whatever is pure, right, and praiseworthy.

God loves you and is always with you. He will be faithful to make a way of escape during your hardship and temptation. "No temptation has seized you except what is common to man. And God is faithful; He will not let you be tempted beyond what you can bear. But when you are tempted, He will also provide a way out so that you can stand up under it." (1Corinthians10: 13)

Jesus was also tempted as a man. "For we do not have a high priest who is unable to sympathize with our weaknesses, but we have a high priest who has been tempted in every way, just as we are-yet was without sin. Let us then approach the throne of grace with confidence, so that we may receive mercy and find grace to help us in our time of need." (Hebrews 4:15-16) Don't forget that He was in human flesh just like us. He had feelings much like we do, but He overcame His temptations without sin. We can draw our victory from Him, so that without shame, we are allowed to come with confidence before God with our needs. What do you think Jesus did when He was tempted? How do you think He escaped from the grips of it? He prayed, fasted, stayed in communion with the Father and confessed the word of God against the devil. Because "the Word of God is living and active. Sharper than any double-edged sword, it penetrates even to dividing soul and spirit, joints and marrow; it judges the thoughts and attitudes of the heart." (Hebrews 4:12) The book of Matthew, chapter 4, gives in detail of how Jesus handled Satan during His time of temptation. With every temptation that the devil dangled in front of Him, Jesus proclaimed the powerful Word of God against it. This is an example for us to follow whenever we need to flick the devil off our shoulder. Confess the Word of God over our situation, knowing full well that WE ARE OVERCOMERS IN CHRIST. In John 16:33 Jesus assures us, "In this world you will have trouble. But take heart! I have overcome the world." He said we would have trouble in this world. But, He also says, "It's going to be o.k. I've been there and I've conquered that for you and now keep your head up and your chest out because when I overcame, you also overcame." Through Jesus we can overcome our trials and maintain a peaceful life.

Satan is real and he means business. I will not exalt him, but I will not avoid telling you that he does have power. And when you give him a little room in your life, he will come in quickly and take more than what you anticipated. He will CONSUME you. It is important not to ever give Satan any room in your life. But, once you have given your heart to Jesus and made Him the Lord of your life, you also have overcome the world and Satan is forever under your feet.

The instant that you come to your decision for Christ, you will have the Holy Spirit of God living inside of you and that power that raised Jesus from the grave in triumph then will live inside of you. You will be born again spiritually. That's what Jesus meant when He said, "YOU MUST BE BORN AGAIN to enter into the kingdom of heaven" in the book of John, chapter 3.

God will give you the authority in the name of Jesus to cast Satan aside and command him away from you. He will give you authority over demons and all evil forces. In Luke 10:19 Jesus says, "Behold, I give you power over ALL the power of the enemy . . ." Ephesians 6:12 tells us, "For our struggle is not against flesh and blood, but against the rulers, against the authorities, against the powers of this dark world and against the spiritual forces of evil in the heavenly realms." "The weapons we fight with are not the weapons of the world. On the contrary, they have divine power to demolish strongholds." 2 Corinthians 10:4 Gods' word is a divine weapon. The name of Jesus is a weapon to take hold of in faith. Prayer, faith, and love are the weapons we need to fight the good fight of faith. It all centers on putting your faith in God. He will be the one to pull you through. He says it's not by might, it's not by power, but by my Spirit. (Zechariah 4:6) The Holy Spirit of God in you (as a born-again believer) will help you hold on to a victorious life in Christ Jesus.

For example, a police officer who has recently become an officer has as much authority over the public as an officer who has been on the job for several years. As long as he HOLDS HIS POSITION, he is in authority no more or less than the veteran police officer. He just needs to learn how to use that authority. In the same way, the Holy Spirit gives the new Christian authority over the devil. God does not give you power over your circumstances but over the spiritual source of your circumstances. As you continue to read God's word, pray, worship and praise Him, and come to know God as your spiritual provider, you will learn how to use your authority against your enemy the devil in the powerful name of Jesus. Jesus is the One Who made it possible.

"Salvation is found in no one else, for there is no other name under heaven given to men by which we must be saved." (Acts 4:12) "God exalted Him to the highest place and gave Him the name that is above every name, that at the name of Jesus every knee should bow, in heaven and on earth, and under the earth, and every tongue confess that Jesus Christ is Lord, to the glory of God the Father."(Philippians 2:9-11) Don't think that Satan doesn't already know that. He has already bowed; he has already experienced his LOSS at the cross. Therefore, he knows that he has to flee in the name of Jesus. When we submit ourselves to God, we can resist the devil and the Bible says, in James 4:7, that "HE WILL FLEE FROM YOU!"

Use the Word of God to speak over the foolishness of the devil. Remind the adversary that HE is the loser. Whenever you know that Satan is bothering you just remind him that according to 2 Corinthians 5:17, "I am in Christ, I am a new creation; the old has passed away, the new has come." Tell him "I will not do what you are trying to influence me to do. Devil, you have been defeated by the blood of the Lamb and I command that you leave, in Jesus name!" Familiarize yourself and memorize the scriptures that will be helpful as ammunition against your enemy. Put them in your heart, and when you need them, they will be there. It's not hard. You will be equipped to pull out the Lord's sword of the Spirit, and God's word will confirm your victory. Confess your victory and you will soon see yourself as the victorious person God has made you to be.

Most importantly, if you want to overcome any kind of temptation, you have got to hold on to the One who overcame. God's word has to be rooted in your heart to bring strength to your soul (mind, will, and emotions) during the hard times.

As you get to know God, you will realize how valuable you are and how important your life is to Him. He will caress you with His presence, love you with His Word, and embrace you with the Truth. Through it all, He will become your strength to resist temptation.

Because I was determined to walk closely to God, it was easier for me to resist temptation. When I needed a friend, He became my best of friends. When silence grew thick in the midnight air, He never left my side. When temptation bore heavily in my mind, He was my refuge and resting place and His Word was there to remind me of who I was in Christ Jesus.

I respected, loved, and most of all valued our relationship as I placed myself totally in His care. I discovered how meaningful every part of my life had been to God. As I read His Word, it became very clear to me that His love was different than any I had ever known. He wanted deeply to be a great part of my life, as He wants sincerely to be the best part of your life now.

I stayed in communion with the Father. Like Jesus, I prayed and in the hour of temptation I was made able to stand strong. It's not hard to pray. It's simply talking to God. There doesn't have to be a lot of decorative or eloquent words. The simplest words from a humble repentant heart will move the mighty hand of the Father across the world.

Although I didn't fast then, I have fasted for different reasons since. Jesus fasted and I believe that He did it to make His body and soul submit to His Spirit. He knew His body and soul were about to stand against the attacks of Satan, but He wanted to be spiritually prepared for the Father's plan.

I will say it again. If you want to overcome temptation, you have got to hold on to the One who overcame. Stay focused on Him. Stay focused on His Word. Think about what Jesus did for you. Think about the sacrifice that He became for you so that you could be an heir of God's kingdom. Think about the Truth of His love for you even to the point of death so that you wouldn't have to spend eternity in hell. Think about the blessings that come with being a child of God. Who can turn his back on this awesome God of love and life only to embrace a god of hate and death? Why walk in the path of darkness unable to see your horrid destination until you arrive? God has a wonderful plan for your life.

Because the pleasure of sin from temptation lasts but a short time, it cannot ever compare to "the crown of life that God has promised to those who love Him" (James 1:12) which will last forever.

The crucial thing here is not to give up on yourself, and most importantly, not to give up on God, Who has waited long and patiently for you. Certainly God will reward you for your obedience and love toward Him. If you make a mistake, the worst thing you can do is waste your time dwelling on it. If you dwell on it, you end up giving too much attention to it and lose your focus on God and your new life. Don't be hard on yourself. Get up, dust yourself off and keep going forward. All things come to pass. Give God room to teach you through His Word. Philippians 1:6 tells us that "He who began a good work in you will carry it on to completion until the day of Jesus Christ." The day of Jesus Christ will be discussed in a later chapter. But, get involved in a Holy Spirit active church, a church that does NOT compromise the Word of God. Make yourself some Christian friends who will pray for you and who you can make yourself accountable to. Renew your mind by studying the word of God that's living and active and sharper than any double-edged sword.

God is always there with you, cheering you on to continue in your goodness. Be diligent and know that He is faithful to be there with you. He knows your weaknesses. He will give you the strength. 2 Chronicles 16:9 states, "For the eyes of the Lord range throughout the earth to strengthen those whose hearts are fully committed to Him." He is faithful to meet ALL your needs according to His glorious riches in Christ Jesus. (Philippians 4:19) From the beginning of time many have rejected God and rejected each other, but He will never reject those who call on His name. In times of trouble, He will be there to comfort you and strengthen you and uphold you. In my past, I have been rejected many times, in many different ways and every time it hurt deeply. If you've been rejected, then I know what you have gone through. I know how you feel. If you've been done wrong, I know how it feels and it's not a good feeling. I have been there and I know that it's a painful hurt. But listen to me. If you go to God, He will meet your needs in every aspect of your life. Just put your faith and trust in Him and He will work things out for you. Your needs for love, affection, acceptance, and security can be met in a godly manner that will bring you a fulfilled life, to glorify the Lord, and bring Him honor. He will bring His rewards with Him. "Behold, I am coming soon! My reward is with me, and I will give to everyone according to what he has done." Revelation 22:12

He has done what He has set out to do; God sent His Son to the cross allowing the punishment to be placed on Him for ALL our sins. He made a way for you to pass from the darkness in your life to the light of His. Don't pass Him up. Don't put Him off. I urge you to take Jesus as your personal Savior. You will never regret taking His love as your very own. When you see Him face to face and here Him say, "Well done, my good and faithful servant," then you will come to realize that the most important issue to Him was your salvation. Look around you. Do you see everybody in your world all concerned about what Jesus did for him or her? No, not everybody is and some people haven't even given it a thought. That's why Jesus warns us to enter through the narrow gate because WIDE is the gate and BROAD is the road that leads to destruction, and MANY enter through it. But, SMALL is the gate and NARROW the road that leads to life, and only a FEW find it (Matthew 7:13-14). God is calling you to come out and separate yourself from this lifestyle. In Matthew 23:37, God the Father says, **"how often I have longed to gather your children (that's YOU) together, as a hen gathers her chicks under her wings, but you were not willing."** Don't worry about what other people might think about you. Let me tell you that what other people think about is not going to get you *into* heaven when you go, and it's not going to take you *out* of hell if you go.

YOU are what He died for. He put YOU first and foremost before Himself. On the day of His crucifixion, when the soldiers led Him away, He let Himself be beaten beyond recognition. His flesh was torn and deeply lacerated from the continuous striking of the whip, constructed with claw-like stones. Every strike of the whip would embed the sharpened edges of the stones into His beaten and bruised body pulling away His flesh. Spitting on this face of God, they pounded a crown of thorns into His brow as they mockingly proclaimed, "Hail, King of the Jews." Everyone watched in anticipation. A few watched in their sorrow as the soldiers hammered the nails into the hands that mercifully healed the sick and the feet that brought liberty to the captives. He said, "Father, forgive them, for they do not know what they are doing." Even then He was releasing them from their guilt. After He had died and was hanging there lifeless, they pierced His side and His forgiving **blood** quickly ran down the splintered cross to us all.

In the Old Testament, before Jesus was born, God required the **blood** sacrifice of animals without defect from a herd or flock for the forgiveness of sins and healing of the sick. Without the blood, there is no mercy. Without the blood, judgment stands alone before God waiting for you and me. Without the blood, God would not have been able to demonstrate His justice. (Romans 3:25-26) Without the blood, there would be no remission of sins (Hebrews 9:22), nor divine healing for the sick (Leviticus 14). But God made Jesus to be the unblemished sacrifice once and for all. *Through **His blood**, He defeated death, hell, and the grave once and forever so that all things on the earth, under the earth, and in heaven would (in all certainty) be destined to remain FOREVER POWERLESS against the "**Atonement**" (the reconciliation of mankind to God).* (Pastor Joel Osteen)

He endured the pain and withstood the shame to deliver you sinless to God. It was as He had said an event that had to happen so that the scriptures would be fulfilled. His will was God's will. He knew what He was doing; He knew why He was doing it, and He knew it had to be done. He was doing it for us. He was doing it for YOU. He submitted Himself to be our sacrificial Lamb of God. He committed Himself to be our one and only Savior.

After 26 years of being gay, I took a step of faith that I had never known myself to take and I'm here to tell you IT CAN BE DONE.

Let me clarify myself about that dream I had of Jesus sitting at my bedside approving my homosexual lifestyle. 2 Cor.11: 14 says that Satan himself masquerades as an angel of light. He is the deceiver and he speaks contrary to God's word. The truth is in the uncompromising word of God. Where there is truth, there is no doubt.

Hell was not meant for God's people. It was meant for Satan and his angels of darkness, but he is trying to take as many of God's people with him as he can. He has refused to understand the love of our Heavenly Father. If Satan had known the motive that God had when Jesus went to the cross, he would have never helped to put Him there. Hate helped put our Savior on that cruel cross, but love kept Him there; His strong eternal love for you.

Chapter 6

Pressing Forward With God

Frank and I were engaged for nine months and went on to get married on my birthday, Nov. 1994. He also had accepted Jesus as his Lord and Savior and with his old life behind him, together we walked down the aisle placing all our trust in God. The new beginning of a life together was worth the start with God leading the way. It has taken adjustments on both our parts, but God has never left us. We've never given up on each other because God has never given up on us.

Christmas of 1996 brought us our beautiful, baby girl, and we named her Querida, which translated from the Spanish language means Beloved. Her middle name is Gregoria, and that is my husband's mother's name. She's always been a blessing of joy to us. She's filled with the love of God and goes around randomly hugging other children. She always has plenty of kisses to give anyone that wants them. She never seems to run out. When I look into her big brown eyes I catch a glimpse of Jesus.

At age three one day while we were exiting a store, I heard her making those familiar smacking sounds that she makes when she puckers up for a kiss. I turned around to find her gesturing for a kiss from a complete stranger, an elderly man sitting on a park bench. Through a child God sends His love.

Two years later, our first born son came. Mr. Cordero was born. Cordero means the Lamb of God. Unbelievably, he was a big package weighing 10 lbs., 12oz. He's a big bundle of love and laughter. He loves to love and be loved. God has given a prophetic word that he will be used to reach many for Christ. I know that God will have His glory.

And last but not least, three years later we had a third blessing. We named him Israel. He follows his dad everywhere. If he's not sitting with him, he's wrestling with him. But Israel is kind and tender hearted.

My husband Frank, I have found, is a man of integrity. His love toward me has always been a genuine kind. It is the kind of love that I never thought a man could possess. He is as sincere as the tears that he cried on the day that I parted friendship with him. I have been told that I'm lucky to have a man who cares as much as he does, but I know that it is Christ in him that causes him to be the best father to our children and the greatest husband to his wife.

You may or may not ever wish to be married; however, that is not the message I have been trying to convey to you. Your decision to accept or reject God's gift of salvation is the main issue because a gift offered cannot be given if it is not received.

There is more to life than what you have already experienced. There is a brighter tomorrow ahead. Words cannot describe everything that God has prepared for you. But one thing is for sure, you are loved.

Chapter 7

Jesus The Healer

Mark 5:24-34 says "A large crowd followed and pressed around Him (Jesus). And a woman was there who had been subject to bleeding for twelve years. She suffered a great deal under the care of many doctors and had spent all she had yet instead of getting better she grew worse. When she heard about Jesus, she came up behind Him in the crowd and touched His cloak, because she thought, 'If I just touch His clothes, I will be healed.' Immediately her bleeding stopped and she felt in her body that she was free from her suffering."

"At once Jesus realized that power had gone out from Him. He turned around in the crowd and asked, 'Who touched my clothes?'"

"'You see the people crowding against you,' his disciples answered, 'and yet you can ask, Who touched me?'"

"But Jesus kept looking around to see who had done it. Then the woman, knowing what had happened to her, came and fell at His feet and, trembling with fear, told Him the whole truth. He said to her, 'Daughter, your faith has healed you. Go in peace and be freed from your suffering.'"

This woman had been sick for a very long time. And I am sure that she was sick and tired of being sick and tired! She had spent all her money on all the medical attention she could afford and still had that sickness in her body growing worse.

When she heard about Jesus, she just knew in her heart that He could heal her from her disease. She heard and she believed. With her faith in what Jesus could do for her, she pressed in to touch Him. Many people were touching Jesus, but He only felt the one who touched Him in FAITH. The Bible says that she PRESSED IN to touch Him. People were in her way, but she PRESSED IN to get her healing. She was FOCUSED on Jesus and went straight to Him as her source. She knew that He could heal her.

Faith will always get Jesus' attention. Faith will always draw power from Him. **Faith in Jesus is what will set anyone free from any disease no matter how long they have had it or how fatal it has become.** And I am speaking a strong line here to cancer and Aids victims. We need to take God's Word seriously knowing that He wants us to take Him up on every word He says.

The doctors may tell you there is nothing else that can be done for you, and let me tell you that is probably true. They probably can't do any more for you than they already have, but JESUS the GREAT I AM says, "I AM YOUR HEALER!" When He comes on the scene of your darkness, that darkness HAS TO FLEE. No sickness from hell can withstand the presence of the Lord. It must bow to the powerful, ever reigning King of Kings and Lord of Lords. Jesus won that battle for His people a long time ago, and the victory remains. He took your sin in exchange for salvation AND your disease in exchange for healing to the **cross**. Nothing has changed. He is still the same King of yesterday, today, and forever. THE VICTORY IS YOURS.

Jesus went around preaching the good news of the kingdom of God and healing every disease and sickness. He healed every disease and sickness that came before Him to be healed in faith. He was on His way to heal the daughter of a man who had come pleading to Him for His healing touch. While the man was still pleading, some friends of his came to him and said, "Don't bother Jesus because your daughter is dead." They were saying that it was too late. Have you ever thought that it was too late for your healing? And you thought, "There's nothing anyone can do for me now not even God. Death is inevitable since I have this life challenging disease. Maybe it's just God's will. I just have to live with the fact that I am certainly going to die." DON'T YOU DARE LIE THERE AND DIE! Jesus the Great Physician can do what no one else can do! He can give you a new start in life that's never crossed your mind. You don't have to live with the FACTS of DEATH when you have the TRUTH of the EVER LIVING GOD on your side that says, **"If you hold to my teaching, you are really my disciples** (disciplined or learned). **Then you will know the truth, and the truth will set you free."** (John 8:31-32) "So if the Son sets you free, you will be free indeed!" (John 8:36) He CAN and WILL set you free! When you HOLD ON to the promises, when you PRESS IN and TAKE HOLD of His cloak, when you stretch out in FAITH, He will feel the power go out from Him, turn to face you and heal you completely, because you believed.

If you were there in those days when Jesus walked the earth, He would have preached the Word to you and wanted for you to be healed of your infirmity, too. He never based His healing of the people on whether they were good enough or sick enough. He had compassionate love and tender mercy for God's creation, which was His every motivation.

You didn't have to be there two thousand years ago with Jesus so that you could have been healed. Jesus hasn't ceased to exist and He hasn't changed

His plan. He is still the same Healer. "Jesus Christ is the same yesterday, and today, and forever." (Hebrews 13:8) He continues to heal people today because of the work He did on the day of His crucifixion.

His death was not the end but the beginning of His ministry.

His work on the cross gave us the victory we needed spiritually and physically. When He saved us, He saved our spirit, soul, and body, ALL OF OUR BEING COMPLETELY!

Before Jesus was even born, the prophet Isaiah, in Chapter 53:5, proclaimed that Christ was "pierced for our transgressions (sins), He was crushed for our iniquities (wickedness or unrighteous acts), the punishment that brought us peace was upon Him, and by His wounds (stripes) we were healed." Let's read that again. BY HIS STRIPES WE WERE HEALED! So that means that He provided healing for us before we were sick. Well, then, "Why am I sick?" you might ask. Your source is the devil. Let me ask you something. Did you really know Jesus before today? Did you know about the wounds (stripes) on His back when you got sick or the blood that He shed as the sacrifice for your well being? Could you have stood up to the devil, with your faith in the promises of God, before he consumed your body with disease? Maybe like many of us, you didn't know a whole lot about Jesus and His divine healing plan, but that's o.k. You're still alive and breathing and you still have a chance to take Jesus up on all He has to offer you.

"Blessed are they whose transgressions are forgiven, whose sins are covered. Blessed is the man whose sin the Lord will NEVER count against him." (Romans 4:7-8) God made a way for us be to separated from our sins. His intentions were to cancel out the sins of the sinner and allow him to walk the rest of his God-given life out in peace and in health. Jesus didn't just bat for first base and then go sit in the dugout. He hit with great intentions and ran to cover ALL the bases before He went home to glory. Those wounds were all about healing US whether it's physical, emotional, mental, or relational.

After Jesus' death, Peter wrote in the Bible that Christ "Himself bore our sins in His body on the tree, so that we might die to sins and live for righteousness; by His wounds you have been healed. For you were like sheep going astray, but now you have returned to the Shepherd and Overseer of your souls." (1Peter 2:24-25)

Like salvation, healing comes through faith to those who will believe. You don't have to work for it; just have faith. Jesus healed the people in the Bible as a result of their faith. He would say to this one "Your faith has healed you" and to that one "Your faith has made you whole." He always recognized the faith they had in Him as He placed healing in their diseased bodies. Some of the sick who went to Him for healing weren't Christians, some weren't even His followers and He knew it. But, He went around healing ALL who were under the power of the devil because they BELIEVED in what He could do. They had never heard Him preach. They had never heard about His kingdom. But, they heard there was a healer in town and by faith they went to Him, BELIEVING for their miracle.

You are special to God. You are a precious creation of His hands. A perfect God made your body in perfection. Your body is important to God. If your body is carrying any kind of disease or sickness, it is not there because God placed it there. He cannot inflict any pain in you when He has already taken it upon His own son. You can place the total blame on Satan. He is the one who came "to steal and kill and destroy." (John 10:10) He caused that sickness in your body. It was either placed there directly from him because he hates you, or it was placed there indirectly through sin. Either way you look at it, it came from the pit of hell and it was meant to take you down.

Jesus came to destroy the work of the devil. He said that He came "that they may have life, and have it to the full." (John 10:10) His plan was to destroy the works of the devil so that you could have life to the full and He did. Mission accomplished!

Early one morning, Jesus' disciples were amazed when they saw a fig tree wither after the powerful words of Jesus had caused it to die. In Matthew 21:21-22 Jesus replied, "I tell you the truth, if you have faith and do not doubt, not only can you do what was done to the fig tree, but also you can say to this mountain, 'Go, throw yourself into the sea,' and it will be done. **If you believe**, you will receive whatever you ask for in prayer."

The measure of faith that God has given you will help develop the health your body needs. Faith, the Bible says, is the "**substance** of things hoped for, the **evidence** of things not seen" (Hebrews 11:1, Gideons Int'l.). The healing that you need is made from this basic matter, this substance, called your faith. It is the evidence or the proof of the healing that you have not seen yet. So where does your proof come from? It comes from the solemn Word of God, the Father.

While snarling, the devil asks you, "Where is the proof that this healing is yours?" Pushing back your chair, as you slowly take a stand, holding up your Bible, as you look directly to heaven, you confidently proclaim, "Here is my EVIDENCE and ALL THE PROOF I NEED; within the pages of HIS WILL AND TESTAMENT, MY FATHER HAS GIVEN HIS DECREE!" OPEN AND SHUT, THE CASE IS CLOSED!

Let's talk about this faith that God has given each one of us. Equipping us with the measure of faith indicates that He starts all believers off with the spiritual faith that they need. Remember that Galatians 5:22-23 tells us that God gives us this faith as a fruit of the Spirit when He comes to live in a new believer. Therefore, we need to keep it alive by feeding it God's word. We need to keep our faith exercised and growing in strength to benefit from it. So just like eating healthy food and exercising your body to make it stronger and keep it developed with firm strong muscles, we also need to take in God's Word and exercise (activate) our faith which will cause it to grow and strengthen for our beneficial use.

Faith comes by hearing and hearing by the Word of God. (Romans 10:17, Gideons Int'l.). Studying the scriptures on your own, listening to faith-filled tapes of the Word, keeping His wonderful promises in your heart and **meditating** on them will help your faith to grow.

When you're sick, you take medicine maybe three times a day. Why not allow God's Word to be your medicine? Take it into your heart. Meditate on it daily. Allow it to bring the strength you need into your body, soul, and spirit. Knowledge of the Word of God going into your ears as you hear it, into your heart (spirit) as you meditate on it, and into your mind as you confess it, will make you whole and set you free. Listen to what God has to say. He is talking to you through His Word.

Jesus said, "If you remain in me, and my words remain in you, ask whatever you wish, and it will be given to you." (John 15:7) With the truth you store in your heart, God will restore your body and soul and spirit. After all, isn't that what Jesus died and was resurrected for—to save your whole being, to make you whole? The Word of God that remains in you will set you free! It brings liberty into your life.

I thank God for medications that help me feel better. I thank God for the intellect of the professional doctors to help my body when it's in despair. But, there may come a time when we need more. We find ourselves in need of more, in need of the Greater Power, Jesus Christ. God assures you that if you seek Him from **wherever** you may be, "you will find Him if you look for Him with all your heart and with all your soul." (Deuteronomy 4:29) "For the Lord your God is a merciful God; He will not abandon or destroy you or forget the covenant" which He made long ago. (Deuteronomy 4:31) If you seek Him earnestly, you will find Him. His compassion is being expressed to you. IT IS HIS WILL THAT YOU BE HEALED AND REMAIN WHOLE RIGHT NOW!

Some people receive their miracle instantly while others wait in faith for their healing. **It's a promise that healing will come** because it has been done. The work of the Lord never fails. Miracles are instant. Healing is a process, and the God of mercy will not forget His promise to you.

Some people remain healed for the rest of their lives but while we are in this world with Satan, he will continue to put up his fight. Sure, it's a fight, but it's a fight that results in victory given to us by our loving Father. Few people lose their healing because God intends for us to be made whole and remain in health. Some go back to the lifestyle of sin from which they were delivered and this exposes them to the devil and the disease they were set free from. As soon as one is back in the enemy's domain, he sets himself up against the attack with all the forces of evil.

But on a brighter note, as a child of God, an "HEIR according to the promise" (Galatians 3:29), YOU ARE ENTITLED TO YOUR HEALING. It is your privilege. The devil may come and in your thoughts tell you that you are not healed and then try to give you some symptoms and say, "See, I told you that you weren't healed. God may have said that He could heal, but He didn't mean you." HE'S ALWAYS LYING, just like in the Garden of Eden. Don't you fall for it, my friend. Hold on to your faith even if the whole earth shakes under you. Don't let the adversary strip you of your faith because of your circumstances. That's what he is certainly after, your faith. We live by faith, not by sight (2Corinthians 5:7). WE LIVE BY FAITH! Life in our body is by FAITH. Our daily walk with God is by faith.

The Bible says that God's will IS for you to be healed and remain healed. *If it were not His will, then Jesus was sinning and acting in rebellion against the Father when He went about healing all forms of sickness and disease. If healing was not God's will today, then the Holy Spirit that Jesus sent among us, after His ascension to be with the Father, this wonderful Holy Spirit is also in rebellion by continuing in the saving and healing work of Jesus.* (Author unknown) "If you love me, you will obey what I command. And I will ask the Father, and He will give you another Counselor to be with you forever-the Spirit of Truth." (John 14:15-17) "He will bring glory to me by taking from what is mine and making it known to you. All that belongs to the Father is mine. That is why I said the Spirit will take from what is mine and make it known to you." (John 16:14-15) And as we pray for each other to receive healing are we too sinning? No, His will is for you to be saved and delivered from disease. Out of His love for you, He yearns to give you what you need. I could never say it enough.

So we hold on to the Word of God and quote out loud those promises that give health to our bodies and life to our beings. Speak out loud the ever-living sharp Word of God. You will be strengthened with every word you say. "The tongue of the wise brings healing." (Proverbs 12:18) It "has the power of life and death." (Proverbs 18:21) "Man does not live on bread alone, but on every word that comes from the mouth of God." (Matthew 4:4) Speak health over your body. I am not telling you to deny your pain or sickness. I know it's real. **I am urging you to take hold of that which is rightfully yours and speak it until it comes into existence.** Speak life over yourself. The power of life and death is in your tongue. When the power of God's word enters into your heart and becomes revelation to you, watch expectantly for that miracle because God is faithful and **the Bible says that He watches over His word to perform it.**

Listen, I have been encouraging you to have faith in what Jesus will do for you and to have faith in the Word speaking it over your diseased body. But, let's back up while I point out to you what has been done on your behalf. I mentioned to you previously that like salvation, healing comes through faith.

But so that one might not ask "faith in what?" I must say, have faith in the sacrifice of Jesus for the salvation and healing of mankind. The significance of the blood from the animals that God used for forgiveness and healing in the Old Testament was an arrow pointing to the top of a hill named Golgotha where a cross stood erect and a Man hung suspended and the shedding of His blood was the last scene of justice that God demonstrated before He brought the curtain down.

The Lord is worthy of our faithfulness. He gave His all for us. Take care of your body for it is a temple of the Lord when "God's Spirit lives in you." (1 Corinthians 3:16) If anything that you did helped bring that sickness within you then STOP, REPENT, and MOVE FORWARD with God, and you will see the reward of the Lord come forth in your life.

I had an issue of blood that not many people knew about. I didn't like talking about it then, but God has healed me since then, and I will give Him all the glory. God healed me after I took His word into my heart because it became so real to me. For seven years, I battled with this frequent bleeding and pain that seemed to worsen over time. The doctor, who I went to, gave me three different tests to check for internal bleeding. He was trying to find out where it was coming from and why. All tests showed no internal bleeding. So he concluded his diagnosis and told me that I was suffering from a torn and inflamed colon. He sent me home with medicine that would nurse the symptoms.

It was around that same time that I had given my life to Jesus and started reading the Word of God. Searching the scriptures, I found that Jesus was not only my Salvation, but He was also my Healer. I found out that the direction of my faith in Him as my Healer and Provider was greatly important. I knew at that moment that God could heal me. I held on to the faith in what He had done for me, and in His timing He pulled me through. **The time I spent filling my spirit with His Word and waiting for my healing to manifest caused my faith to grow and my heart to become closer to Him.** My faithful Savior had provided the healing my body had so desperately needed.

"My son, (daughter), pay attention to what I say; listen closely to my words. Do not let them out of your sight, keep them within your heart; for they are LIFE to those who find them and HEALTH TO A MAN'S WHOLE BODY." (Proverbs 4:20-22) I know that God can heal. He has in every way proven Himself to be faithful. He does what He says and does not back out of His word. **He will give you life and health on the condition that you pay attention to Him, listening closely to what He says and keeping His words in your heart**. You have to seek His Word before you can find it. "Worship the Lord your God, and His blessing will be on your food and water. I will take away sickness from among you, and none will miscarry or be barren in your land. I will give you a FULL LIFE SPAN." (Exodus 23:25-26) **"Why die before your time?"** (Ecclesiastes 7:17)

"In the beginning was the Word, and the Word was with God, and the Word was God." (John 1:1) God and His word are equal.

Jesus said, "out of the overflow of the heart the mouth speaks." (Matthew 12:34) When the Word of God enters into your heart, your most inner being, **so does God**. When the Word exits from your heart and through your mouth, so does the very **existence of God**. WHAT POWER, WHAT GREATNESS!

Psalm 103:2-5 declares, "Praise the Lord, O my soul, and forget not **all** his benefits, who forgives **all your sins** and heals **all your diseases**, who redeems your life from the pit and crowns you with love and compassion, who satisfies your desires with good things so that your youth is renewed like the eagles." What a large inheritance a child of God has. He heals ALL our diseases and forgives ALL our sins. There isn't one sin that He does not forgive, nor is there one disease that He does not heal. Since you are the beneficiary, I suggest that you find out from your Bible all that God has provided for you. You already know about His forgiveness and divine health, but God's love brings much more to you.

Maybe you've heard someone say, "Well if it's God's will that I be healed then He'll heal me. If not then I'll just have to stay this way." WRONG! All scriptures indicate that it IS God's will for His people to be healed and saved. The Bible rules out "if it's Gods will." There is no IF about it. Stand your ground in faith and receive your promise of healing as you take Him at His Word. He wants for you to take Him at His word and believe Him with all your heart.

James 5:15-16 says, "The prayer offered in faith will make the sick person well; the Lord will raise him up. If he has sinned, he will be forgiven. Therefore, confess your sins to each other and pray for each other so that you may be healed." In this passage of scripture, why did James find it necessary to combine healing and the forgiveness of sins together? In Matthew chapter 9, Jesus healed a paralytic immediately saying, "Your sins have been forgiven." Why did He heal and forgive the paralytic at the same time? **Because sin left unforgiven gives root to sickness and disease.** Jesus came to restore and redeem that which was lost. That was His mission. And as He healed that paralytic, He pulled that sickness out of his body from the roots by forgiving him of sin.

God gives grace to the humble and will come near to you if you will come near to Him. James 4:10 tells us, "Humble yourselves before the Lord, and He will lift you up." **In 2 Chronicles 7:14, the Word says, "If my people, who are called by my name, will humble themselves and pray and seek my face and turn from their wicked ways, then will I hear from heaven and will forgive their sin and will heal their land."**

There is nothing more important that God the Father would rather do than to have a meaningful relationship with you. He wants to be your God, if you will choose to be His people. He wants to be the Father you've never known a Father could be. He wants to be your best friend if you choose to have a relationship with Him. He wants to be your source of health if you will believe in Him. This Great Father of Heaven stands eager with open arms to receive you into His refuge. He will provide for you a meaningful and fulfilling life from here to eternity.

"Forget the former thing; do not dwell on the past. See, I am doing a new thing! Now it springs up; do you not perceive it? I am making a way in the desert and streams in the wasteland."(Isaiah 43:18-19) He is doing a new thing in your life!

Chapter 8

Jesus Will Return

1Corinthians 15:51-52 reveals, "Listen, I tell you a mystery: We will not all sleep (die), but we will be changed-in a flash, in the twinkling of an eye, at the last trumpet. For the trumpet will sound, the dead will be raised imperishable, and we will be changed."

1Thessalonians 4:16-17 says, "For the Lord Himself will come down from heaven, with the trumpet call of God, and the dead in Christ will rise first. After that, we who are still alive and are left will be caught up together (a rapture) with them in the clouds to meet the Lord in the air. And so we will be with the Lord forever."

The rapture of the church (all born again believers from every denomination) will happen so suddenly, in the twinkling of an eye, or as fast as the flash of a camera. That's pretty fast. Those who are being called to meet the Lord in the air will be the only ones able to hear the sound of the trumpet at the time of Christ's arrival. The world won't even know of it until they are faced with the after affect evidence of all the missing Christians.

Ask yourself if you are prepared spiritually to go with Him. Where will you be and what will you be doing upon His return? What will you do about His love and His resurrected life for you?

What a reunion! We get caught up to meet the One Who died for us and get reunited with our loved ones who died in Christ before us. Our bodies will be changed into glorious bodies like His. No more battles with sin, pain, or disease. We will finally be in our new home celebrating our victory and safe from the tragedy that is to come.

In Luke 21:34-36 Jesus tells us, "Be careful, or your hearts will be weighed down with dissipation, drunkenness, and the anxieties of life, and that day will close on you unexpectedly like a trap. For it will come upon all those who live on the face of the whole earth. Be always on the watch, and pray that you may be able to escape all that is about to happen, and that you may be able to stand before the Son of Man."

Immediately after He takes us to be with Him, the times of tribulation will commence. The Bible warns us of the signs of the end of the age (end of the world) which are slowly unfolding now and include the seven years of tribulation.

According to the Bible in the book of Mark, the signs of the end of the age are events that have been taking place and continue to happen. In chapter 13, Jesus explains all that is to take place before the day of His return. For example, wars, and rumors of wars, brothers killing brothers, fathers killing children, children rebelling and having their parents put to death, people hating each other because of Jesus, handed over to local councils, and taken before governors as witnesses for Christ. Many events that are happening now are the signs of our Savior's return. However, many other tragic events will happen to the world economically, financially, and in leadership and governmental issues before the end of the age as foretold in the book of Revelation. Nearly two thousand years ago, our ancestors were carefully awaiting Christ's return. Tell me how much more, this day, should we be preparing ourselves that the time has drawn MUCH nearer? HE WILL COME SUDDENLY AND UNEXPECTEDLY. We need to be prepared.

1Thessalonians 5:1-10 states, "Now brothers, about times and dates we do not need to write to you, for you know very well that the day of the Lord will come like a thief in the night. While people are saying, 'Peace and safety,' destruction will come on them suddenly, as labor pains on a pregnant woman, and they will not escape.

"But you, brothers, are not in the darkness so that this day should surprise you like a thief. You are all sons of the light, sons of the day. We do not belong to the night or to the darkness. So then, let us not be like others, who are asleep (not reborn spiritually), but let us be alert and self-controlled. For those who sleep, sleep at night, and those who get drunk, get drunk at night (not being watchful). But since we belong to the day, let us be self-controlled, putting on faith and love as a breastplate, and the hope of salvation as a helmet. For God DID NOT appoint us to suffer wrath, but to RECEIVE SALVATION through our Lord Jesus Christ. He died for us so that whether we are awake or asleep, we may live together with Him."

In Revelation 16:15 Jesus warns, "Behold, I come like a thief! Blessed is he who stays awake and keeps his clothes with him, so that he may not go naked and be shamefully exposed." The Bible tells us to clothe ourselves spiritually, being self-controlled, putting on faith, love and hope as spiritual armor. (For more on armor see Ephesians 6:10-18). We need to clothe ourselves with the righteous one, Jesus Christ, to be able to stand firm in the faith in all that we do and through all that comes against us so that we will not find ourselves ashamed at His coming.

In Matthew 13:24-30 continuing in v.37-43, Jesus tells us a parable: "The kingdom of heaven is like a man who sowed good seed in his field. But while everyone was sleeping, his enemy came and sowed weeds among the wheat, and went away. When the wheat sprouted and formed heads, then the weeds also appeared."

"The owner's servants came to him and said, 'Sir didn't you sow good seed in your field? Where then did the weeds come from?'"

"'An enemy did this,' he replied."

"The servants asked him, 'Do you want us to go and pull them up?'"

"'No,' he answered, 'because while you are pulling the weeds, you may root up the wheat with them. Let both grow together until the harvest. At that time I will tell the harvesters: First collect the weeds and tie them in bundles to be burned then gather the wheat and bring it into my barn.'"

"Explaining this parable Jesus said, "The one who sowed the good seed is the Son of Man. The field is the world, and the good seed stands for the sons of the kingdom. The weeds are the sons of the evil one, and the enemy who sows them is the devil. The harvest is the end of the age, and the harvesters are angels."

"As the weeds are pulled up and burned in the fire, so it will be at the end of the age. The Son of Man will send out His angels, and they will weed out of His kingdom everything that causes sin and all that live in evil. They will throw them into the fiery furnace, where there will be weeping and gnashing of teeth. Then the RIGHTEOUS WILL SHINE LIKE THE SUN IN THE KINGDOM OF THEIR FATHER. He who has ears, let him hear."

Jesus came and planted His word in the hearts of many. He went abroad spreading the gospel of the kingdom of God throughout the earth being an example for the people to follow. His work was completed at the cross, and He went home to sit at the right hand of the Father in heaven. But, His seed continues to be planted by evangelists, pastors, prophets, teachers, followers, neighbors, friends, and family members who may have tried to talk to you about a wonderful Jesus Who died to bring you life today. This seed is, at the present time, in your possession. If you, being as good ground, receive it, and allow it to take root and sprout, you will have the life that God has prepared for you.

God can and will bless you with a new life in a way beyond your thoughts. His thoughts, the Bible says, are not like ours. "For my thoughts are not your thoughts, neither are your ways my ways. As the heavens are higher than the earth, so are **my ways higher than your ways and my thoughts than your thoughts.**" (Isaiah 55:8-9) He has a good plan for your life, full of hope and a boundless future. Just take Him at His word. Trust Him. He is trustworthy.

God, the Father, can see more in you than you will ever see. You have been CHOSEN. He has **"chosen you to be saved through the sanctifying work of the Spirit and through belief in the Truth."** Hold your head up. God has made you worthy. You are worth the precious blood of His Son. You are what stirs up great compassion in His heart. God loves you just the way you are, but He wants to take you higher than where you are now. He looks past all the failures and mistakes, beyond all the circumstances and situations and finds you as precious and beautiful as the day you were born. **God loves you with all that He is**. His eyes look upon you with such a countenance of deep love as never expressed before.

Nothing in this world could be worth going to hell for. Even if you were to say that you've already sold out your life to Satan, or you're too far into the occult, 1John 1:9 says, **"If we confess our sins, He is faithful and just and will forgive us our sins and purify us from all unrighteousness."** Consider God's great everlasting love for you. There is no reason why anyone should perish when a worldwide invitation to salvation has been handed out to ALL.

Jesus is in love with you. You are the apple of His eye. There is nothing else that He would rather do than to see you, your family, and your friends in heaven with Him to partake and enjoy what He has prepared especially for you.

As a friend, I tell you that I've been where you are, and I encourage you to leave those things in your life that will cause eternal separation from God. No one will be there with us when we stand before Him and have to give account for the life that He gave us. Because of His love for you, He waits with open arms to receive you as His very own.

The Lord says, "Today is the day of salvation." To put it off would be your greatest mistake and most sorrowful regret. Hebrews 3:7-8 states, "So, as the Holy Spirit says: Today, if you hear His voice, do not harden your hearts . . . ."

Before Jesus left this earth, He said in John 14:1-4, "Do not let your hearts be troubled. Trust in God; trust also in me. In my Father's house are many rooms; if it were not so, I would have told you. I am going there to prepare a place for you. And if I go and prepare a place for you, I will come back and take you to be with me that you also may be where I am going."

Jesus concludes by saying, "I am the Way, and the Truth, and the Life. No one comes to the Father except through me." John 14:16 He IS the way to heaven. There is no other way by which we can get to heaven except by going the direction of the cross, following the trail of His blood, and allowing the Holy Spirit to guide us. There is no other name by which we must be saved but by the precious name of JESUS CHRIST.

If you would like to receive a new life, to become a child of God, to be able to walk away from homosexuality and to be given a place in His kingdom, this prayer will help to lead you through the threshold of the Kingdom of God. Read it through, then pray it out loud as a confession of faith, and God will honor you while all of heaven rejoices. May God richly bless you as you walk with Him. As the father of a princess once said in *Princess Diaries,* one of my favorite movies, "The key is to allow yourself to take the journey".

Prayer to receive your Salvation

Thank you Father for your son Jesus, who I now proclaim as my Lord and Savior. I believe that He died for me, that you raised Him from the dead and that He is seated at your side. Jesus, I repent from this life and confess you as the Lord of my life and I ask you now to come live in my heart. I renounce the lie that You have created me or anyone else to be a homosexual. I agree that in Your Word You clearly forbid homosexual behavior. I choose to accept myself as a child of God. I turn my back on the devil and everything that he represents. Lord, give me a new spirit and the strength to walk with you one day at a time. Help me to live by your commands and to learn your ways. Thank you, Lord, for making me a new creation. In Jesus' name I pray. Amen.

Read your Bible daily to get to know God.
Pray and spend time alone with God.
Find yourself a Holy Spirit filled and led church and get involved.
Tell someone about the decision you made to live for Christ.

www.dontwanttobegay.com
Victoria, Texas 77905